Time
PASSES ON

Brenda
Friendships makes
memories Thanks
for the memories that
Are yet to Come
                                    Lance
                                    11/24/16

LANCE FIGGINS

PAGE PUBLISHING, INC.
New York, NY

First originally published by Page Publishing, Inc. 2016

ISBN 978-1-68348-969-6 (Paperback)
ISBN 978-1-68348-971-9 (Hard Cover)
ISBN 978-1-68348-970-2 (Digital)

Printed in the United States of America

To Paula Berg without her it would not have happened. I could not have had a better partner in the publication of these books. It's because of her work and dedication on the first two books they made it to printing. She did all the pre editing all the computer work before during and after the editing. Also the total cover design of each book and a number of other things that I did not have time to do. Thank you so much Paula. I could not have done it without you.

There are again a number of people I need to thank They would be the test readers. Anna Kelly Palladio, Dawn Zarin, Lesa Verdin, Jennie Bymark Roy, Julie Monroe, Linda Wagner Nelson and Jody Skejskal Johnson thank you very much for your advice and encouragement. Next would be my parents Marvin and Darlene Figgins for their support. The same for my brothers Scott, Kevin and Todd again thank you. Next would be my son Joshua thank you being a great son. Last of all Paula's children Shaelynn Marie, Nate and Ben you really make Paula's life easy. Be good to her she is a fantastic lady. I hope I did not leave anyone out. If I did, I'm sorry, and thank you.

Missing Slippers

Co-written with Paula Berg

The crime of the century of Grand Rapids's fame.

The ruby red slippers were stolen, what a shame.

(Somebody took them and slipped out the door.)

Is it possible the crime could have happened this way?

Could the Scare Crow, with his intellectual brain,
designed the crime of Grand Rapids's fame.

Imagine the Tin Man, with his heart adore, came
in and chopped through the museum door.

Did the Cowardly Lion who is coward no
more slip in through the broken door?
He picked those slippers up and walked away.

The Good Witch of the north could not
control the flying monkeys that day.
They all got loose and flew away.

The escaped Flying Monkeys met them at a predetermined site.
Helped them with their criminal flight.

(Thieves) and slippers have never been found
and are believed to still be around.

Although this caper did not happen this way,
it has not been solved to this day.

Someday the slippers may be found and
brought back to our hometown.

They belong in the museum for us all to
see and for our town to share.

Beautiful Lady

Hey, lady, beautiful lady.
So deep in thought.
Am I in trouble?
I pray that I'm not.

Every time I hold you.
I look into your eyes.
I can see something new.
Something there for me.

I can see the love in you.
The love that is there for me.
Do you see the love in me?
The love that is there for you?

Even though we are a thousand miles apart.
I can feel you next to me. I feel it in my heart.

As I sit here, I'm thinking about you, I can feel it too.
I can feel that you're at home and thinking about me.

The love we share can span distance and time.
Distance and time are only there if we don't care.

Every time I leave your side, it is just what I do.
I am just trying to get back to you.

I love you, girl.
It's all I want just to be with you.

Should I Try

End of the week, I am headed home.
It's been a couple years, and I'm still alone.

There have been ladies in my life.
So far no one I wanted to make my wife.

There's a new girl from my hometown.
She's really sweet, this I know.
We spent a lot of time together.

There've been times I thought of a ring.
I'm not sure if I'm ready for that.
I really don't want to get hurt again.
I'm sure she would take the ring.

She says I'm really special to her.
She spends a lot of time with me.
Whenever I'm home, she's there for me.

She's a great cook and a fantastic lover.
I always call ahead to invite her over.

We spend as much time as we can together.
I guess I should make her mine forever.

Someday this could come true.
Until then I'll just stay true.

Walk Out the Door

Yes! It was you back then.
That was just, a few months ago.
You were the world to me.

Everything I thought, it could be.
Why did it not work for us?
Why is your head filled with doubt.

How could you give up on us?
Was it that easy for you?
What did you want from me?

So I sit and wonder why?
Can I love again?
My head is spinning.
Filled with questions again.

You were always first with me.
I don't want to set you free.
All the plans are just memories.
From the day you left me.

How can I make it go away?
I don't want it anyway.
I can't live like this anymore.
I watched you walk out the door.

So I sit all day in love.
With a memory of love.
You're the one who walked away.
From the love so strong in me.

Have you found someone new?
Was it worth what you put me through?
I watched you walk out the door.
I'll remember that forever more.

Reach

All the dreams we dream.
Are they real? Should we scream?
There are so many dreams.

They seem really like I can touch.
I reach in the dream but you're just out of reach.

So I reach again, I stretch, I grasp, you're not there.
I grab nothing but air.

I try and try you're not there.
I'm screaming in this dream. I beg, I plead.
You just laugh standing there, just out of my reach.

I can't reach. Why are you just out of reach?
I plead, I beg, I scream again.
Then I try again and again.

You stand there just out of reach.
You laugh again; I plead, "Come to me"; I beg, "Just take one step."

Then I can reach you.
I stretch again; you move just out of reach.

Is this a dream or is it true?
Why can't I get to you?
I'm reaching and stretching too.
You stand there and laugh again.
I can't reach.

Year Ago

It was a year ago that I broke your heart.
It was a year ago that I tore us apart.

I can remember exactly what happened on that terrible night.
The night I broke your heart.
The night I tore us apart.

I remember what happened next.
What happened next is what happened to me.

I remember the tears I shed.
I remember what you said.
When I told you I was going back to her.

For I relive it each and every day.
It's a day I can't forget.
It's stuck in my memory; it will not go away.

I still regret that day.
I regret it in every way.
The pain is still here.
It will not go away.

Someday I may see you again.
Maybe then I'll be free.
Maybe we'll be together again.

Rugged Beauty

Central Ontario today, land of bear rock and majestic pine tree.

You see the scars as the glaciers push through.
As tons of ice, covered this land.

Beaver and the moose were abound.
As the voyagers explored this land.

As you look across this land.
The rugged beauty seemed to be God's plan.

The Great Lakes is a visual too.
Cold and clear and oh so blue.

Did the Vikings discover this land?
There are facts that say they did.
That they were here long before.

It is a wonder to behold.
This land can be so cold.
The rugged beauty is a must see.
The land of rock and pine tree.

Mom

This is to my mother; listen to what I have to say.

I didn't come with instructions, but you loved me anyway.
Thank God there was a no-return policy.
Would I be here today?

Although I can't be with you, I'm all these miles away.
You made my life worth living.
Filled with love and happiness.

You hugged away the nightmares and kissed away the tears.
You were always there for me throughout all those years.

For this I am so grateful, and I will love you unconditionally.
Thank you for giving me life.

This comes from my heart, and I thank God above.
I hope and pray you have a fantastic Mother's Day.

Guy for You

I was thinking about this today.
I have something I'd like to say.

Do you want to keep running around?
I should find someone new?
If you're ready to settle down.
I think I'm the guy for you.

I know this guy is ready now.
To settle down, you're the one in life for him.
The one that should be his wife.

I just want you to be the one.
Standing next to me.
All I think about every day.
This is the way it should be.

This is the way that it was one day.
We played and loved every day.

Please tell me and be true.
Have you found somebody new?
If you have, then I'll go away.
Then I won't be the guy for you.

I Wait and See

As I sit on the mountainside.
Gazing the other side.

Looking for the thing I seek.
Takes me back to years gone by.
In the mountains on the side.

Did a mountain man sit right here.
Doing something similar?

Did an Indian brave pass by.
Or did a hunting party camp nearby?

As I try to hunt these hills, my eyes search all around.
Looking for most anything that might be found.

How about a grizzly bear?
Are there any close to here?
Or maybe a mountain lion could be hiding over there.

Why do I think like this?
History is really neat.
There are so many things, that history does not seek.

In the mountain near the peak.
All of the beauty here to see.
If you would hunt like me.
Wildlife is here just waiting to be found.
Scenery is so beautiful, streams, trees, and hidden lakes.

Rough and jagged are these peaks.
Only the strong can survive.

I can see why the Indians wanted to keep us out.

I sit on the mountainside.
Trying to decide.
Should I wait right here or walk to that ridge line there?

Maybe what I seek.
Is just over there.
Will it come to me? Or must I go look and see.

Life has its ups and downs.
Should I wait or should I seek?

If I wait, I could grow old.
If I move, will it find me?

Only time will tell.
As I sit here on the mountainside.
My mind travels all around thinking of things I've done.

Diamonds

I was looking at my pictures today.
I saw one that made me sad right away.

The picture I saw was a ring.
I bought for you so long ago.
It brought me back to a time and place, I did not want to go.

To a time that you still loved me so.
I can't believe how it made me feel.
What we had was so strong, so real.

Every time I looked at it.
My eyes got wet.
I couldn't see the sparkle in front of me.

It was just your diamond ring.
The ring that meant everything.

About the love I thought was strong.
About the love I have for you, I thought you loved me too.

The ring I got was just for you.
It showed how I felt for you.

Everything I did in life.
All I wanted was to make you my wife.

I guess that will never happen now.
I'll keep your ring and love somehow.

Every time I look at it.
I'll remember what you meant to me.
Every time my eyes will get wet.
Every time I will not see.
The sparkle in your eyes when you see it.

Live, Love, Laugh

There's this girl I knew a-long time ago.
She was so pretty I wanted her so.
She left one day.
Never returned.
I thought about her over the years.
I was conceited back then; I never looked back.
That was a mistake I made, I now realize that.
She's very outgoing and gorgeous too.
I think about her every day or two.
This girl I know is now a friend to me.
Will there be more? I'll just wait and see.
I live for today and all it can be; tomorrow is just a dream to me.
My life is so full of ups and downs.
Every day is a smile followed by frowns.
So until the day I decide to settle down.

I live by a rule it's simple to me.
Live life.
Laugh often.
Love with your heart.
Forgive and forget.
Life's too short.
This rule can work for you too.
Live, love, laugh—it's easy to do.

Chances Are

Is there a chance I could be happy again?
Can I find someone new?
Someone I love?
The way I love you?

There is a chance.
A very little one.
The way I love you is second to none.

The chance I'll take, to be happy again.
To let someone new have a piece of my heart.

The little piece that is left.
To let her in.
Will be hard to do.
The way that you tore me apart.

If I do try to let her in.
There's so little left that piece of my heart.

All that you left, when you left me.
Was so little no one can see.

I sit here and try to rebuild what's left.
That little piece, I protect what's left.

If she comes in and tries to replace.
I think she will lose the entire race.

What you left for someone new.
Is too small for anyone, but you.

If you should ever return to me.
Please bring back the rest of my heart.

Although it is yours, you can have it for life.
The only way is to be my wife.

Life Desire

Can you love a girl and desire another?
Can your heart work, if you desire another?

This question is still fresh in my mind.
My heart is here, my mind is there.
It will not let me unwind.
It won't let me find the time.

What can you do if you love two?
Is it possible to be true?
The love I have for one and the other.
Can I love one and desire the other?

I'm not married, it's not like that.
The girl I'm with is in love with me.
She is very special to me.
The girl I desire says she loves me, but she can't be with me.

Is it possible to survive?
Is it possible to stay alive?
If one knows but not the other.
Can I love one and desire another?

Loving Verse

Roses are red, violets are blue.
That's not the way to say "I love you."

The way is just to say the words she wants to hear.
Speak from the heart, make it oh so clear.

Of all the things you can say to her.
A simple verse is all she wants to hear.
A simple saying "I love you" could bring
tears to the eyes so beautiful.

Remember the things are best in life.
When you include your loving wife.

Remember the verse she wants to hear.
Say it loud and also clear.
Make sure she knows every day.
That you love her in every way.

Never allow her to close her eyes.
Without giving her the loving verse.
Tell her you love her every day.
With a little bit of luck and "I love you,"
she'll be yours and always stay.

From Me to You

I think I've found her at last.
The girl I've looked for, as time passed.

She's the one I want in life.
The girl I wanted all of my life.

She's everything I want in life.
The one girl, I want to make my wife.

She's tender, she's loving.
She's special to me.
She's all I need her to be.

The way she looks at me.
Makes me the man I want to be.

So if you're as lucky as me.
Hold on tight, don't set her free.

I think I have found her at last.
The one I wanted for life.
The one, the only girl for me.

So make her the woman she wants to be.
Treat her right, give her life.

Tell her you love her.
Make her your wife.

Played

I felt like I was being played.
She said something to make me feel that way.

Why does she do things like that?
Tells me she loves me. Then does a thing like that.

She was my world, an angel in my eyes.
Then she left and moved in with another guy.

These things are so very hard on me.
Then she says she's still in love with me.

My head is swimming in thoughts and words.
All my thoughts are somehow backwards.

I know what I should do.
But I know I love her too.

For weeks I haven't heard from her.
Then she sends a text.
My thoughts go back to her.

It isn't fair; she is messing with my head.
At this rate I'll soon be dead.

I know that I still love her.
Hopefully she'll someday prove her love for me.

You spend your time trying to figure out why.
Is this happening? Can it be fixed?
Usually there is no fix. Just go and live your life.
To survive to love another day.

Time Passes On

You spend your day alone.
You want so much to pick up the phone.

All you do all day is think about her.
She said back off or we're through.

So you bury yourself in your work.
Your mind goes to her every time you feel like a jerk.

You want to send her a message or maybe a call.
But you think it would be better if nothing at all.

You miss her so much you want to cry.
You know you can't; you're a tough guy

You wonder if she's doing okay.
Inside you pray she's miserable anyway.

You wonder how long this feeling will last.
You know in time this too will pass.

You sit and wonder if she is missing you too.
She has friends that hate you.

You think maybe you should find someone new.
Instead, you pray she's missing you.

You spend the day counting the hours.
You think maybe you could send her some flowers.

You sit and look at a dating site.
You know no one but her can make you feel right.

You say, "Forget it, I'll find someone new."
You know inside she's the one for you.

You find someone that looks like her.
Your heart won't let you be with her.

Time goes on and on and on.

Pain Away

I woke up with a jerk.
Like someone I knew was getting hurt.

I don't think it was a dream to me.
It feels so real. How can this be?

Has it ever happened to you?
It's like you can feel their pain and misery to.

It's weird and kind of strange that I should feel someone else's pain.

It feels like someone I love or did.
It feels like its stronger that just a friend.

It's still there, but now it feels more like they're thinking about me.

It must be someone that I've loved or love.
I feel it more in my heart, I think.

It started out in my head and migrated to my heart.

If I ever figure it out.
I'll be in contact without a doubt.

It feels like there in so much pain.
They cry each day what a shame.

All I know it's driving me insane.
I'm pretty sure it's a she.
I can feel she's in love with me.

I wish she would contact me.
Maybe I can help her deal with her misery.

I'll say a little prayer today.
To help her on the way.

To do what she needs to take the pain away.

Certain Guy

Do you ever sit and just start to cry.
Then you can't figure out why.

Then you realize you've been thinking about a certain guy.
It is that guy that makes you cry.

Am I that guy you dream about?
Am I that guy you cry about?

Do you ever wonder why?
That you just start to cry.
What can I do to convince you why?

That I am that certain guy.
That you miss me, and that is why you sit and cry.

Should I give up or should I try?
Are you in love with that certain guy.

Freedom

As I sit in this cab.
I look around; why would a guy consider this life?
Consider this home?

It is my home over three hundred days each year.
It's where I work, live, and play.
Every day of the year.

Playing sounds kind of strange to you.
Yet, yes, playing is what I do.
I put my skills against all things.
Weather, traffic, and other things.

I miss the people I leave behind.
Loved ones and friends are strangers to me.
I spend more here than I do with you.
I think about them every day I'm gone.
Girlfriends the one I always depend on.

If the life I lead would yesterday be.
An outlaw or cowboy.
A wagon train master or a wilderness guide.

I love what; I do it's not strange to me.
Think about this. Would it be strange to you?

It's a freedom that is so hard to explain.
It lives in your heart, it is never the same.

The friends I meet and friends they are.
We all live the same. Every day of the year.

We travel across this great nation of ours.
It's a land to behold; it's breathtaking too.

I can't explain, nor do I want to.
It's something that grows inside of you.

Girlfriends my life we are a team.
Think about what I say.
It will become clear to you.

Can Never Be

I contacted an old lover the other day.
Just to see if she was okay.

We message back and forth for a while.
Then I said something that I thought could make her smile.
I ask her if she still loved me.
This is what she said.
This is how she replied to me.
I will love you forever.
I think about you every day.
Missing you is the price that I must pay.
I will love you forever for all eternity.

For you were my life.
You were the world to me.
Loving you was easy.
Losing you was the hardest on me.

This is where I am now.
Its gets harder for me every day.
Sitting close beside him with his arm around me.
Wishing it was you sitting here beside me.

Kissing him as I close my eyes.
Standing in front of him.
Praying it is you when I open them.
Praying it is your lips that I'm kissing.

I close my eyes and pray every day.
It is you lying beside me.
It is your touch that I feel.
It's just you that I miss every day.

I know deep inside.
I'll never feel that again.
For you are the love that can never be.

I hope this answers your question.
Of how and what I feel.
Do I still love you?
Yes, and for all eternity.
For you are the love.

That can never be!

Explore

There is nothing more beautiful to me.
Than the Rocky Mountain scenery.

So rugged is this place.
From the snowcapped peaks.
To the forested slopes.

The rock formations and sheer rock walls.
Rugged beauty covers them all.

There is so much to see.
More than a lifetime to cover them all.
Two or three lifetimes would not cover it all.

It's a wonder that I can spend as much time as I do.
Getting to explore, hike, and do what you can to see this land.
It's too magnificent not to see.
If you can, you must explore this land.
Enjoy these mountains to the end.
It's all there just waiting for you.

Give Me Back the Key

If you love me, come and be with me.
If you don't give me back the key.

My heart has an empty place.
Without you to fill the space.

My heart doesn't know which way to go.
Without you to tell me so.

I miss your smiling face.
I need you to fill that space.

My heart says, "Come, be with me."
My mind says, "Let me be."

I miss all the things you did with me.
The way you said hello to me.

It still puts tears on my face.
It feels like such a disgrace.

Every time I think of you.
I hope you're missing me too.

I think about you every day.
I don't know what to say.

I wish you'd come, be with me.
Or just give me back the key.

Is this just a dream to me.
For I know you set me free.

Someday it may come true.
Until then I'll just stay in love with you.

Heart's Desire

I really like you, I really do.
Why must I change for you?
It isn't fair this thing you do.
Saying I must change for you.
Change is hard on me.

Why don't you change for me?
My ways you say are not right.
That is just your insight.
All these things are studies, you see.
Really, honey, they're not me.
Of all the things you say I do.

There's just one thing I do for you.
I promise I would be true.
To the heart inside of you.
You are a special kind of friend.
The one that I want to be with until the end.
To hold you tight when you cry.
To kiss the tears from your eyes.

Being with you is my heart's desire.
Hold your hand and be at your side.
Loving you my life entire.

Feeling Inside

How can this happen?
Can anyone explain it to me.
It's happened before and now again to me.

It happened about a month ago.
It happened again just a couple days ago.

It seems like I was dreaming about you.
At the same time, you were dreaming about me.

I'll try to explain how it felt to me.
When I was dreaming about you.
You were dreaming about me.

Is it possible to be in someone else's dream?
At the same time they're in your dream.

I could feel the pain you're in.
The pain felt so real, the pain I could feel.

It felt like you were crying in your bed.
It felt like you were dying in your head.

Your pain was my pain.
I can feel it inside.
Sometimes strong like I'm dying inside.

Someone please explain to me.
How I can feel what she's feeling inside?

Someone please explain it to me.
Can she feel what I'm feeling inside?

Power of Love

Love is the greatest feeling as long as it's given and received.
It has to be that way. It takes two to play.

The feeling is stronger than any man.
It picks you up to the highest places.
Put you down, you'll think you're under the ground.

When it's good, you're in heaven, there's nothing better.
When it's bad, you're just a mess; nothing can be worse.

If it's given and not received.
Days haunt your nights and nights haunt your days.

You spend your time trying to figure out why.
Is this happening? Can it be fixed?
Usually there is no fix. Just go and live your life.
To survive to love another day.

Still Looking

We met on a dating site.
If you don't look like your pictures do.
You have to buy me drinks until you do.

I don't know what else to say.
People are just strange that way.
There are many single girls out there.
The one I'm looking for is out there somewhere.

If I'm lucky enough to find her.
I'll hold on tight and protect her to the end.
Make her happy, keep her safe.

Let her know she's all I need, she's all I want.
Treat her like a queen should be.
Take her out for all to see.

This is just a dream to me.
A dream that I want for me.
To find the one I'm looking for.
To make her happy, loved, and more.

Thinking of Me

I sent you a message, you never sent one back.

You said you loved me that has never changed.

Then you said I should find someone new.

What the hell is wrong with you?

Can't you see why I'm a mess?

What the hell is the rest?

Have you flipped your lid?

Have you gone off the deep end?

Has your depression got you down?

Are you just goofing around?

Is it fair, this kind of deceit?

Messing with my head is not neat.

If I move on, would you be really happy?

Or would this just prove that you could have been happy?

I know I can find someone new.

I'm just scared it would destroy you.

All of this is in my head.

It's still there, when I get out of bed.

Every morning I think of you.

I just hope you're thinking of me too.

Stars at Night

You sit and look at the starts at night, praying she's doing all right.

You look over a lake so blue, hoping she's missing you.

You try to clear your mind of her.

Your hearts stronger, it holds on to her.

You sit and look at the forest green; she is all you've ever seen.

You sit one night and stare at her ring.

You can't believe she rejected the thing.

You wake in the morning filled with might.

You know you've survived another night.

You go for a walk and look at the sky.

You pray she's not with another guy.

You hope someday you'll see her again.

To give her a hug and love her again.

Seeing Him Through Her Eyes

There he was holding her hand.
That should be me holding his hand.
I can't believe I let him go.
He was right there, I loved him so.
I should be there, I still love him so.
He's with her and now I have to go.
He begged me to let him in.
I was scared to get hurt again.
All I can do is pray someday.
He'll remember me and want to stay.
Today they walk past me.
He didn't look, I ran away and cried alone.
I guess there's nothing left for me.
To die a little more each day and let him be.
But I still love him so, and I know that he let go.
I'll cry some more and remember him so.
I can't believe I let him go.
I made a mistake when I forced him away.
I can't believe I made him stay away.

Bury Deep Away

There's this trucker buddy of mine.
He had trouble with his wife one time.
I walked with him.
Talked with him.
Ate with him.
Trucked with him.

I gave him advice one time.
I told him if he truly loved her.
You can forgive her and work through the pain.
Together in love you can do most anything.

You must forgive her, but you must lock that pain away.
You must bury it deep inside and never
again let it see the light of day.

That you must forgive and forget and love her until this day.
You must make sure you keep that pain, and it is buried far away.

I told him if you truly loved her.
You can forgive most anything.
If you do, you could never bring it up again.

I'm glad to see they worked it out.
They are still together today.

It is fantastic to know they're still together and in love to this day.
That he was able to lock his pain away.

A love like theirs is made in heaven above and
should be there for all of us to see.

Place I Eat

There's this little place I stop and eat.

All the people are oh so neat.

There is a waitress there, if she sees me drive in.

She orders my breakfast right there and then.

I always try to sit at the same table.

My coffee and water are waiting for me.

I was late one day she said, I don't know what you want for lunch.

Was all she had to say.

My coffee and water were there anyway.

She's a great waitress and friend.

I let her read a poem now and then.

This little place is neat.

The people there cannot be beat.

The food is excellent too.

I highly recommend this place to you.

The Covered Wagon just can't be beat.

Traveling Dreams

I sit here and think of days gone by.
Why did I do the things I did and why?

Where do I go from here?
What's the point of life from here?

What's next? I ask myself.
I've changed jobs and everything else.

Is there someone out there looking for me.
How can I find her? How can this be?

All the things I've done so far.
I've always provided a good life.

Lately things are changing real fast.
Is it good luck? Will it last?

I have driven and worked hard all my life.
So hard, it cost me my loving wife.

For her is all that I did.
Why oh why did she do what she did.

Can this be in the cards?
Was it her choice? She had a voice.

I did what I did for us, you see.
Yes, for her and, yes, for me.

The kids are grown and are leaving home.
It was our time.
To live our life and to live in our home.

We have what we wanted.
She could have quit her job and went with me.
We could travel and do what we want.
To stop some place and look around.

To just be together to never part.
These things are still in my heart.

There they will stay and be with me.
Like I said before it's just a dream to me.

So girlfriend and I will travel alone.
Dream, our dreams and never go home.

She will always remain with me.
Tucked away safely inside of me.

My dreams will stay and remain with me.
Until the day my heart will finally set me free.

Heart

How can this happen? How can it be!
I thought you were in love with me.
Was it that easy for you, to forget about me.

You said that I was your world, your everything.
Just like that you changed your mind.
Just like that you forgot about me.

Is your heart really that hard? Is it like made of stone?
Don't you feel a little inside? Don't you wonder why, don't you cry?
I thought I really was your guy.

How can you face your day?
Don't you ever just think about me?
Do you ever just sit there and start to cry?
Do you think of what's happening inside?

To me you were my everything.
All I could think of every day.
It's what kept me going all day.
Knowing you were there waiting for me.

Now things have changed for us, it seems.
Now all I have is broken dreams.

The days have changed, you now live in my heart.
Even though we are apart.
As times pass, this will stay, you'll live in my heart all of my days.

Dispatch's Calls

Dispatch waited to call.
Until it was just about too late to load.
Then they call now!
You're going to work.
Most of the night.
What a jerk.

It's like they just wait for you to make plans.
That way your girl has the right to get mad.

There are times I feel it's on purpose.
It's like they know what's going on.
Just as you make plans and then they call.

Your plans for dinner went tumbling away.
You call your girl with the bad news today.
She tells you it's not a big deal.
Just go work is all she says.
You can tell by the tone in her voice.
You better leave, she's really peeved.
If you try to say anything, she will just get mad.
So you leave for the truck, feeling bad.
Knowing she is at home alone and sad.

Angel

I think I had a dream last night.
Long dark hair and bedroom eyes.
She was there in front of me.
I had to look twice, what else could I see?

As I sat there staring at her.
I got another surprise.
A golden halo filled my eyes.

Was this an angel standing in front of me.
I just sat there mesmerized and staring at those bedroom eyes.

Then she spoke and said to me,
"Follow me I have another surprise."
As she turned to walk away,
I could see her wings folded up carefully.

She turned back then and beckoned to me.
To follow her to my surprise.

She took my hand and said, "Listen to me.
God has sent me to watch over you.
You have a special gift.
I'll protect you so you can see.
All the things you have to give."

The last thing she said to me,
"The one you love is an angel like me."

I woke up then and looked around.
She was nowhere to be found.
As I sat there, it came to me.
It filled my heart, it set me free.

All the things I have to give is love, respect, and kindness to her.
The poetry is there too.
It's there for all of you.

There are many angels in my life.
I have always picked the wrong one, to be my wife.

So make sure you always think twice.
Make sure the angel in your life.
She could be there in front of you.

Give her all you can be.
Grow up and be a man.
She can fulfill your every need.
She will be all you need.

There and Back

I travel the country.
I travel alone.
Just girlfriend and I.
I get the inspiration to write these poems.

The places we've been to.
The things I see.
The people I meet are all different to me.

This beautiful country of ours is spectacular to see.
In so many ways.
From mountains to oceans to deserts and seas.

We've been to Florida and to Maine.
From Washington to California and in between.

We traveled the country to there and back.
So many times, I don't need a map.

There are times I think girlfriend knows where to go.
She turns by herself before I know.

About ten more years, it is for me.
Then maybe I'll retire just girlfriend and me.

Morning Feeling

I got up this morning feeling down.
Didn't know why.
Thought I would just leave town.

Headed outside to meet the day.
Decided to go and play.

Got my car and headed east.
With no particular place in mind

Ended up on the North Shore.
Parked the car and started to walk.

As I walk, I started to think. It was getting late in the day.
I sat on a rock and just watched the lake.
The waves were breaking.

I started thinking of you again.
It's been a long time.
I thought I was doing fine.

As the sun set, my mind went to you
Not knowing what to do.
Why do I think of you?

It's been a long time, but you're still on my mind.
It just isn't fair. It been a long time.

Come to See Me

I sit here and watch the sun come up.

Take a sip from my coffee cup.

She is still asleep and tucked safely in my bunk.

The sleeper part of this blue truck.

She had to see me and spend the night.

What does she see in a man like me?

She is so sweet, she is too nice.

I love it when she drives to see me.

I spend all my time driving this truck.

Someday maybe with a little luck.

I can quit driving this truck.

She does this quite often, and it's really sweet.

There are places we often meet.

It would be nice to just take her with.

What I haul is just too dangerous.

Everything I haul can burn or explode.

I'm in danger on every load.

Someday I'll quit this life.

Then I'll make her my wife.

Hidden

I sat today feeling okay.

Then I started thinking of you.

I started thinking about the day we met.

What we did is so hard to forget.

Why do I still feel this way?

How can I forget?

I am with someone new.

Someone that loves me, someone true.

On these days, it's so hard to do.

To be with her and think of you.

I try to hide it deep inside.

She can tell I'm not there.

There is something bothering me deep inside.

She can tell, I'm not where I belong.

My mind travels back in time.

To a place I don't want to be.

To the time you were with me.

Yesterday is gone away.

Why won't you just go away.

How can I still want to be with you.

The way we were upon that day.

All these things keep happening to me.

Just like you're still here beside me.

All I can do is pray someday, you'll set me free.

Until then, I'll just be this way.

I'll keep it hidden inside me.

Until This Day

I went for a ride the other day.
I was on a mission, you might say.

I had something I needed to do.
To find a way to forget about you.

I found the place I was looking for.
A quiet place to think about what I had to do.

The day had finally come.
To move on and enjoy my life.
Try to find someone new.
Someone that would love me too.

So I sat and thought about what I had to do.
As I sat on the bank and thought about you.

I started with the text messages first.
I read as I deleted them.
The pain was there, it was getting through.

Yes, I knew what I had to do.
With one swipe, they were gone.
Now started the missing you.

My eyes got fuzzy, my throat got thick.
The pain was there I thought I would be sick.

I tried the photos next.
I didn't think it would be like this.
Every delete brought another tear.
Every delete brought more fear.

My desire was to keep a few.
Was not sure what I should do.
I made an album just of you.
I kept a few and deleted you.

All the time thinking of you.
Deleting you was something I had to do.

This is the hardest thing I ever did.
Giving up and walking away.
I didn't quit until this day.

Love Inside Me

I thought about what she said to me.
About a love that can never be.

Although this is what I think about what she said to me.
She will never see what I think about the love that can never be.

She is my life's desire.
Her soft touch set me on fire.
I have thought about her so much.
My body missed her loving touch.

I miss all the things we will never do.
The places we won't go.

I miss her soft lips and her firm embrace.
I miss her smiling face.

I miss the way she said hi.
I miss it so much I want to cry.
For me it was just so special, just to hear.
It meant to me, I miss you dear.

I guess what she said is true.
The love we had was so true.

As for a love that can never be.
What she said and what I feel.
Will always be held close and stay forever inside me.

Transformer

The American dream is different for everyone.
Some want to be a rich.
Some just want to survive to live day by day.

Mine is simple as simple as can be.
I just want a lady to stand next to me.

This lady I know is unique in so many ways.
She is there for me to get through the day.

This lady is a transformer you might say.
She can look different so many times a day.

Every morning she looks to see, what is the plan.
Then she changes for the demand.

She can dress down for work outside.
She can dress fine, for dinner and a glass of wine.

She can look great like we are having our first date.
Or be fantastic and hold on to my arm.

So we can walk together, and I can show my pride.
Just as if she was my new bride.

Yes, a transformer is what she is to me.
She takes pride in what she brings to me.
I take pride and show her my feelings constantly.

Traveling Prayers

Girlfriends loaded, and we are ready to go.
Once again, it is that time, it's time for me to go.

This time we are running late.
I don't mind, I spent extra with that girl of mine.
I can make up the time when I hit the interstate.

Time at home is never enough.
There's always more than I can do.
That's why it's so hard for me to leave you.

To leave you with everything there is to do.
Makes me feel guilty for leaving you.

This job is hard and demanding too.
It's hard on me, it's hard on you.

Hopefully someday, the day will come.
When I'll take you where I go
Until then I will pray.
That day will come.

As I travel across this land.
I think of you mile after mile.
It makes me sad I do not smile.

One thing I know for sure.
You always pray for me and my safe return.

It's your prayers.
That get me through.
It's your prayers they bring me back to you.

River Deep and Blue

I went down to the river, the beautiful river deep and blue.
When I got to the river, I took a deep breath and thought of you.

I took another breath and walked into the water.
Just to swim to the other side.

When I got to the middle, the current took control.
As I fought the mighty river.
I slowly lost control.
As I slipped beneath water.
All I could do was think of you.

I'll never again taste your sweet lips or look into your eyes.
Just remember that I love you and please, honey, do not cry.

I'll be missing you and the love that we shared.
I'll be okay.
I'm headed to the other side.

Now I am here at your side, love, although you can't see me.
I will always be beside you to protect you, to get you through.

I pray you forgive me for the mistake that I made
and remember that I always loved you.

Just remember how much I loved you.
How I begged you that day not to go.
Please, honey, don't cry for me.

I'm a lucky guy.
I had the love of a lifetime in the time I spent with you.

Never Again

You are everything I wanted in life.
You are my friend, my lover, my wife.

For you were the reason I existed.
For you I would give all of this.

You were where I belonged.
You were my life all day long.

For you I would do anything.
For that you wore my ring.

You were my day and night.
You were my guiding light.

I thought you were happy then.
I guess he convinced you again.

I hope everything works for you.
For you will never again wear my ring.

Never again will you look into my eyes.
Never again will I be there for you.

Never again will you be my wife, my lover, or my friend.

Man You See

Your soft touch and warm embrace.
Always seems to put a smile on my face.

All I want to do the rest of my life.
Is spend it with you as my wife.

You are everything you ever could be.
You bring out the man I want to be.

Loving you is my calling in life.
My goal is to make you my wife.

To treat you like a queen should be.
To be your prince I want to be.

To honor the woman in you is for me.
For you to honor the man in me.

All of this can only be.
If the love is there and allowed to grow.
For love is the key.

For all I am is the man you see.
All I want is the woman before me.

Just Us Two

Every love story is different.

I like ours the best. It started one day in April, this I must confess.

Why are we apart now? Can it be fixed?

Is there anything left? That we can fix it with?

Are you really happy? What will you do?

Could we be together like we used to do.

The plans we made keep going through my head.

As the time passes by, they will soon all be dead.

Just like the love we had, this too will be dead.

I still remember the love we shared.

We thought it would never change.

I remember the last night we had, felt like it always did.

The feeling of you wrapped in my arms was like love made for two.

I left in the morning, had things I had to do.

I guess there was something bothering you.

I wish you would have said.

It feels like a long time but it's been only months.

Love like ours comes once in your life.

It was made for just us two.

There are different ideas that there's only one.

I truly believe you were the one for me.

It think it felt like that to you too.

Laughter Can Fix

The day we met you asked if I could stay the night.

I told you I had to go. I could not stay with you.

The next morning, I called you looking for a cup.

You said, "Get over here, I just made a pot."

We talked all morning, we really get along.

I make you laugh, that's the key to love.

Laughter can fix most anything.

That could start you wondering.

What love and life is about.

You never get to serious.

You take time to laugh.

There are other things we can do.

I can't wait for summer too.

There are funnier things to do.

Be Unsaid

I like to write these poems.
They just flow out of me.

It's more a calling; that is the way it feels to me.
Of all the things I've done, this is by far the best.

I hope you enjoy them.
It's said I'm a romantic, I write about love.

It's what I feel on these day. It flows out of me.
It comes from my heart, that's where it should be.

Love is a fantastic thing. Better than all the rest.
If it's good, you feel like you're the best.

Every time you have a fight, remember what I say.
Be careful of what you say. It can never be unsaid.

Tore Apart

I saw her yesterday.
She waved to me.
I wanted to stop, to talk to her.
Most of the time.
I'm scared to try.

All I can think of is just why.
There's no reason to feel this way.
I still feel it every day.

I talked to her one night a long time ago.
She said, "I just don't want to be."
You're not here with me.
You drive that truck, that's what you do.
I tried telling her, it was for you.

She said, "No, that's not true."
You're always gone in that truck.
I don't want to be alone.

Loving her was my life's desire.
Loving her was all it could be.
She filled me each and every day.
With the desire to work this way.
To provide the things we needed in life.
To give these things to my loving wife.

She still left, and we are apart.
Somehow that's still breaking my heart.
Someday I'll meet someone new.
Maybe she can repair my heart.
The same heart, that my wife tore apart.

Fill With

There's a girl I met the other day.
I think she's great in every way.
She has a way of reading my mind.

Some days, that is really just fine.
Sometimes I just get in trouble.
Maybe I should just run on the double.

All I know is I care about her.
So many things I cannot tell her.

Is there a chance I'll fall for her?
I'm really scared to get hurt again.
That is why I won't let her in.

There are times I think I should.
Just buy a ring and let her in.

If I do, what would follow?
Maybe a smile, maybe tears.
I just don't know if they are mine or hers.

So for now it will remain the same.
Loving her is not a game.
She is too sweet to play a game.

I can't hurt her, it would not be fair.
Yes, I love her long brown hair.

She has the most gorgeous eyes.
I can't help but stare at them.
A mischievous smile and a silly grin.

I think I'll just hang on and go for a ride.
Take my time and see what's next.
I'm really sure she can rebuild my pride.

Loving her would be easy to do.
I'm so sure it would be real cool.

She has a way to put me at ease.
Even to put me onto my knees.

A knee is something I'm not ready to do.
If I don't, I'm probably a fool.

I know I think about her every day.
There are days that's all I do.

Loving her would be an easy thing.
Yes, I know I should buy that ring.

I know that I'll let her in.
I bet I'll see that silly grin.
After she reads this, that mischievous smile will appear.

Those bedroom eyes could fill with tears.

Love or In Love

I sit here tonight in a state of wonder.
Thinking about all you have said to me.

I would like to know if you love me.
Or are you in love with me?

I'm starting to think there is a difference there.
I have discovered the meaning.
There is difference between the two.

You can love most anyone.
Like your mom and dad.
Your best friend or even your neighbor too.

To be in love that is what I seek from you.
To be in love is to know there is no other.

You can think of just that one.
You can be with another if you choose.
But the one you love will lose.

To be in love with the one you're with.
Is the key to a full life of joy and happiness.
If you find the one you're in love with.
Do what you can to convince them of this.

That is the only way to be truly happy every day.
It's a wonder and such a joy.
The happiness will bring the joy.

I guess what I'm saying to you.
If you're in love with me, let me know.
If you just love me, let me go.

Close Your Eyes

Close your eyes and picture this.
A mountain meadow covered with mist.

As the sun rises through the trees.
The dew will sparkle on the leaves.

With daisy and butter cups growing there.
Wild mountain grasses, color everywhere.

Close your eyes and picture this.
A tropical lagoon with water so clear
you can see the colors everywhere.

Tropical fish red, blue and green
the prettiest thing you have ever seen.

A tropical island is for you and me.
Love, peace and tranquility.

The mountain meadow is our home.
Beautiful is the scenery.
Peaceful for when you are alone with me.

Close your eyes and picture this.
You and I engaged in a kiss.
Traveling, loving, being together.
Building a life, loving each other.

Look to the future what can you see.
An old man, is it me.

Sitting there with tears in his eyes.
The tears are for you.
For he is remembering,
the one true love of his life from days gone by.

I Guess

I don't know what to say.
Why should I feel this way?
I found out the truth today.
I still love you anyway.

You've been lying to me.
Telling me he's just a friend.

I guess I'm still in love with you.
I don't know what to say.
Why do I love you still today?

I found out the truth today.
I guess I love you anyway.
I hope and pray you realize one day.
What you had, what you let get away.

As the days have passed by.
The love I had will not die.
I will hold it deep inside.

Hidden from sight, always there for just me.
Tucked away in my loving memory.

Tomorrow Ever Come

Why do I let you treat me this way?
What is so special about you anyway?

You're not there when I needed you.
You're not there anytime.
So I ask again, what's so special about you?

There are lots of ladies out there.
Lots of them who would love and care.

So why do I sit and wait for you?
Is my love that strong for you?

I have tried to date again.
To find someone that would be there for me.
Someone that would be more than a friend.

Every time I hug or kiss them good night.
I close my eyes and picture you.

I have a lot to give to one.
A loving husband for anyone.

Ladies love to be romanced.
That is something I love to do.

To flirt and make her feel real good is something I like to do.
To hold her hand and drink champagne.
To cuddle in front of a fire.
To fill her heart with love and desire.

All these things I love to do.
All these things I did with you.
So why do I wait for you?
I can find someone new.

I think tomorrow or another day.
Maybe I should start that day.

If I find someone new.
Someone who loves me just like you.
What do you think I should do?
I can't waste my life waiting for you.

So yes, I think it's about time.
Time to get you off my mind.
I really hope you find what you want.
I don't think I was the one that you want.

With all the times I've tried in vain.
To help ease the pain.
To get you in my arms.
To convince you with my charm.
Looks like tomorrow is the day.
Will tomorrow ever come?

Tranquility

I sat on the shore of Lake Michigan today.
The waves are spectacular, a wonder to see.

Rolling, crashing, and water spray.
I just sat and enjoyed the day.

With the wind in the trees and wildlife abound.
There is so much to be found.

Mother Nature is a wonder to me.
Just think about it, so much to see.

With all the fantastic wonders there are.
Try to get out and enjoy it or just take a ride in the car.

From the forest, to the lakes, to the mountains,
To the plains, the deserts and canyons—will all self-explain
It's all beautiful in its own way.

Enjoy the wonder of nature as often as you can.
You won't be unhappy, you may even understand.

One Call

Why is forgetting someone you've loved so hard to do?
It's the worst kind of hell it seems to be impossible to you.

You can spend days it seems to put them out of your head.
All it takes is the message from her. Then I have to start over again.

A message, a call, is all it takes.
Just let that happen and you start to shake.
It's like all the good times come back again.

So there you are sitting and wondering why.
Was there a good reason? You're just wondering why!

So you start all over. Trying to straighten out your brain.
Knowing all the time that most of the thoughts will simply remain.

You feel like you're just beating your head against a wall.
While inside you're praying for just one more call.

If that call comes, what will you say?
Will it be forgive and forget on that day.
Maybe some revenge is all she'll get that day.

Beauty of Nature

The beauty and tranquility of the Caribbean Beach.

Is a wonder and something beautiful to reach.

The splendid beauty of the Rocky Mountains just knock me down.

Peace and tranquility abound.

Nothing on earth can compare.

The rugged beauty of the mountains out west.

From snowcapped mountains to clear mountain streams.

To the calm peace of a mountain lake.

The beauty of nature is for all to see.

I hope you have the time to enjoy this like me.

Girlfriend

Why do I live the life I do?
Maybe because I love what I do.
Girlfriend and I travel these roads.
It's a lonely life.
The life I choose.
The highways and byways we travel alone.
It's what I do, it's what I love.
I spend my days staring around.
Looking at the world through the windshield
and going from here to there.
Girlfriend and I are getting old.
Over a million miles, she'll have real soon.
That's over two-round trips to the moon.
At this rate, she'll be worn soon.
Replace her I can never do.
She been too good, she's been too true.
She's never let me down even at forty below.
She runs the roads, she always does fine.

She and I are a pair, you see.
Just like it should be.
I know her noises and vibrations every day.
It's like a lover you see.
It's the same every day.
We will be together to the end.
She's better than most; she's my friend.

Canyon and Park

The Gallatin Valley south of Bozeman Montana.
Gateway to paradise, gateway to heaven.

The scenery is spectacular to see.
But the wildlife is extraordinary to see.

From the mighty moose to the grizzly bear.
Gray wolf, buffalo, and elk are there.
The mule deer, whitetail deer, and antelope abound.

From snow-covered peaks, mountains and meadows,
to grass-filled valleys a wonder to see.

Around the corner, another surprise: Yellowstone
Park, a sight filled my eyes.

The canyon the park, I cannot describe.
The wonders of nature and the beauty of nature's surprise.

This part of our country is a must see.
The pictures do not give justice to the.
The naked eye is all I mean.
The beauty is there, it's far too hard to describe.

Moved On

Am I waiting on something that can never happen?.
Have you moved on?

Is that a star I wished upon.
Is it really just laughing at me?

Were you ever really there?
Did you love me? Did you care?

Why do I sit and think?
Why do I wait for you?

I could be with someone new.
Someone who cares.
Someone better than you.

Many things have come and went.
Time together time we spent.

Where are you now?
Not with me. Not right now.

There are things I can't forget.
Things you said. Things you meant.

What can I do for us now?
Do I wait? Or do I move on?

Love Is

Why do I love you?
Let me count the ways.
Was a poem written long ago.
Is correct in so many ways.

There are many kinds of love.
They are all correct in their ways.
The love I have for you is all there is here today.

The things you said made me think today.
That's why I'm still with you and haven't run away.

The things I feel are so confusing, my heart goes every way.
My mind says something, my hearts goes the other way.

It leans this way, then it goes that way.
The things I feel change, the day is here to stay.
Why can't I just bring back yesterday?

I wish I could say what I feel and what you meant to me.
I try, and it changes, and everything goes
back to where it was earlier today.

Do I write these words of love and try to
stay, in the middle of each day?
My heart says just love this girl and forget yesterday.

The things I feel are confusing.
My feelings are here to stay.
I love you now and I'll forget the things from yesterday.

Love Forever

You said you were hurt, and you said you were scared.
You said you have lots to figure out in your head.

I'll wait for you to decide. I love you now.
You know that. I'll love later; I'm sure of that.
I'm a patient man.
Your number will remain on my favorites where it should be.
Just in case you should decide you want me.

I love you, honey, and I always will.
You said that you still loved me.
I'm so happy that you said that as it should be.

You know deep inside you belong with me.
I'll make you happy until eternity.
These are not just words to me.
It's a promise I'll make to you from me.
Please, honey, listen to me.

Your my life, and you should be my wife.
I know this sounds like a poem to you.
Read the words; they are meant for you.

You are all I think of now.
Come to me!
I'll make it even better somehow.

I'll give you the world, that's what you mean to me.
I love you now and forever, you'll see.
Please, honey, don't turn me away.
I'll love you forever until my dying day.

Why

I tried to contact you and asked.

I called and left a message and asked.

I want to look into your eyes and ask.

You tell me to move on, but it's always a message.

I asked you to say it face-to-face.

But you won't.

I know I hurt you, and I wonder.

Our love was strong and you know.

We belong together and you know.

All I do is sit and wonder.

I love you still and I don't know.

I can't get you off my mind. Do you know?

I'll love you forever and always it seems.

All these things are in my head, I would love to ask you.

WHY?

Sunken In

Well, I think it's finally sunken in.
You really don't want to try again.
I don't believe what you say.
You're confusing me worse every day.
Do you really want me to go away.
You say you're still in love with me.
Then why are you not here with me?
There are so many things we wanted to do.
Now you say you don't know, what you want to do.
I wish I really knew.
What was going on with you.
All the things you have said.
What is going through your head.
Like you're not happy where you're at.
There is something I could do about that.
I have listened to what you have said.
I have read every word.
Then I read it over again.
I hope you find what you seek.
You should find it eventually.
Although I still wish it was with me.
You deserve to be happy.

Hanging On

Why am I hanging on to you?
You said that you were through.
Then you'll send me a message or two.

Sometimes I'll send one to you.
Tell you something that could work.
It seems you're just like me.
Hanging on to something that should be.

Our love was an epic story.
One with love and all its glory.

Then one day I made it go away.
I was scared of what you meant to me.
You cried then said you would survive.

I had to stop that night.
My throat got tight, and my vision got blurry.
I spent the next month thinking about you.

I made a mistake of this, I know.
I talked to some friends about you then.
They all said what an idiot I had been.

I'm not sure to this day.
Why I said, what I said on that day.
You were what I wanted in life.

Months later, I wanted you for my wife.
What is the hold you have on me?
I just know what you meant to me.

You were my world, my life back then.
You were my everything in the world to me.

Hopefully someday you'll see it my way.
Until then I'll just sit and pray.

Weather

I was listening to the weather radio.
They were talking about a tornado.

A few minutes later, I saw it over there.
Thank God it was moving away from me.

I was somewhere I didn't want to be.
A few miles later, it started to rain.
At the same time the wind started to blow.

I had to slow down and drive kind of slow.
I couldn't see the road for the rain and the blow.

As it lightened up, I started to gain speed.
I really felt the need for speed.

I'm so glad I got out of there.
I really didn't want to be right there.

I guess this is just another adventure.
That I'll keep in my memory.
That's where I think that should be.

Superstition Mountains

Superstition Mountains of Arizona are beautiful still today.
They would be easy to explain.

With the exception of Geronimo, Cochise, and
the lost Dutchman fame.
Apache gold and the mysteries surround the
Superstition Mountains of Arizona today.

Where is the lost Dutchman mine?
Or the fabled Apache gold?
Is there really a canyon filled with gold?

The lost Dutchman mine is still a mystery today.
It has never been found. Can it truly exist? Or is it just a myth?

There is Geronimo and Cochise, famous as all the rest.
They know these mountains better than the rest.

I would love to spend time there looking at the
history and mysteries that abound.
Who knows maybe the mine could be found.
Or maybe the Canyon of Apache gold.

Amazing Eyes

I had a dream about you last night.
It woke me up in the middle of the night.

I sat then and looked at your pictures for a while.
As I did, I noticed your smile.

I noticed and remembered other things.
Your sensual lips that I once kissed.

Your beautiful legs that I miss.
As I looked, it dawned on me.
Your eyes are really what I miss.

I just sat and stared at you.
I think your eyes could look straight through.

I looked at every picture I had of you.
I kept coming back to a certain one.

I think I stared at your eyes.
You have the most amazing bedroom eyes.

Although your gone, and we are through.
I'll keep a couple pictures of you.

I hold on to a memory or two.
That's all I get to keep of you.

Here to Stay

It's morning again, I'll be all right.

I've survived another night.

I think I'm getting stronger every day.

I pray these feelings would just go away.

The sky is as blue as my eyes.

It looks really cold outside.

My head is working trying to figure this out.

My heart is still broke without a doubt.

How can a man feel this way.

At my age, I should have turned and walked away.

I sit here with tears in my eyes.

Thinking about her is no surprise.

I know inside these feelings will never go away.

My love for her is just too strong.

It's simply here to stay.

What You Have Done to Me

I spend my days so sad and blue

Thinking only of loving you.

Every day is the same, just thinking of you.

Days run together, every day is the same.

You're in my dreams both night and day.

I see you in visions when I turn out the lights.

I see you in stores every day.

I have to blink twice to make you go away.

It's been so long since I held you tight.

I can't believe that you're doing all right.

I'm a mess, a terrible sight.

I'm so glad you're doing all right.

The days go by, I'm thinking of you.

I pray all day, you're thinking of me too.

You said I was your world and your everything.

Now I just pray you're remembering.

I can't believe, what you have done to me.

Cry Alone

I had a dream about you last night.
Oh my god, what a pitiful sight.

You sat in your room all alone.
You tried to pick up the phone.
You pushed the button to place a call.

Then you push the button to end that call.
You dropped the phone and cried all alone.

Was this just a dream to me, or is it reality?
Is it possible to dream a dream in someone else's head.

Was it a dream, or was it something really real?
Is there something more you're hiding inside.

I guess your pride got in the way.
Of the happiness you could have today.

Maybe someday your pride will step aside.
Maybe someday you'll be happy inside.

Until then you will just cry alone.
Maybe then you can pick up your phone.

In This Guy

Was I just a toy to you?

Someone to toss when you were through?

I'm so sorry, but I feel for you.

A love that was so strong and so very true.

That is what I have for you.

I'm not sure what I'll do.

Should I wait or move on too?

I think I should just sit and wait for you.

I have but one life.

Will it take that long.

For you to realize that I'm near.

For you to forgive and forget all your fear.

I guess I'll move on and not wait for you.

The love I carry deep inside.

Will keep my fire burning for you deep inside.

I hope you realize what I'm thinking is true.

That my love will never die.

It will live forever in this guy.

Looking Over Me

Dedicated to Anna M. Bennett

In 1994, Anna broke her back. She has fought the pain
and depression that comes with such a terrible injury.
In February 2015, I was flipping through Facebook and
learned of this. Her back had gone out or locked up on her.
She was in terrible pain. I sent her a prayer message
and then sent this poem to her privately.
After I read it, I really like it. With her
permission, it's now for you all to see.

I have an angel looking over me.
I'll send her to you.
Just to take a look and see.

If there's anything she can do.
Maybe she can take the pain away.
You'll get better day by day.

She can slowly take the pain away.
If you listen to what she has to say.
She has helped me every day.

I'm sure she can help you too.
Just make sure you take it easy on what you do.

I'm also praying for you.
I hope you're praying too.
It works mysteriously.
It can work for you.

New York Scenery

When you think of New York.
You think of the city all of the people.
In one big city to some the skyline is very pretty.
Upstate is oh so neat.
A lot of nice people for you to meet.
With mountains, trees, hills, and more.
Upstate New York, I could really adore.
Lakes and swamps, rivers and streams.
It feels like home.
So much to see and so much more.
There's so much scenery to explore.
Just pick a spot, there's something there.
You might just enjoy the beauty of a tree.

It Will Happen

I pray for the day.
You come to me and say.
I made a mistake that day.

I hurt you this, I know.
I even told you so.
I begged you to stay.
I asked you over and over that day.

To stay and love me.
That I would keep loving you.
You just turned and walked away.
It hurt so bad on that day.

Now the time has finally come.
That you would say, you still love me.

I knew it would happen someday.
I loved you until yesterday.

I found someone new.
She loves me more than you.
So all I can say.
I am happier than yesterday.

I hope that you're okay.
And you find love someday.

Dream

I love you, girl, I love you, I do.
Maybe so much I can't get over you.

My days are lonely now.
When I think of you.
Why did I do the things I did.
I can't take them back.
I wish I could.

I love you girl, I love you, I do.
I'll spend my life just loving you.

God gives you one love of your life.
This is the one you should make your wife.

I lost the love.
I lost my life.
I lost the girl.
I lost my wife.

I lost the chance that I had in life.
That beautiful girl.
That beautiful wife.

The beautiful life we could have had.
It's now just a dream that I had.

Someday I might be happy again.
The love of my life is gone, I know.
That dream of a life of love still lives in me.
And will remain for eternity

Dedication to Rebecca and Adam

I was already in trouble when I met him.
He became my lover and my friend.

We were like fire and gas.
Put us together things could explode.

It was tragedy on what happened next.
We enabled each other quite a bit.

Then one day God had to choose.
He brought him home.
Left me alone.

I had a choice to make.
To change or follow soon.

To this day I miss him.
For he was my lover and my friend.

His birthday comes every year.
It's a day I love and fear.

I try to remember all the good.
Scared the bad will invade to soon.

As I sit and think about you.
The tears soon come as I miss you.

I know someday we'll be together again.
For now I hope not soon.

I have to live and love again.
I will always keep this day.

Just for you and your memory.
For it's all I have left of you.

The love we shared and how I cared.
For I will always be right here.

On the day I love and fear.
For I will always keep you near.
Held in my heart, we'll never be apart.

I miss and cry for you.
You're at peace, and I love and miss you.

Faith

My angel was there last night.
She said, "Everything will be all right."

She said, "Your plans are looking great.
Be careful what you do.
You might make a mistake or two."

"Everything is looking great.
Remember what I say.
There's a reason she went away."

"Don't make that mistake again.
Everything will be all right.
Remember what I said."

"God sent me here for you.
Just keep track of what you do."

"Everything will be all right
Just keep your faith.
You'll survive and it will turn out great."

Ashamed

I had a dream last night; it filled me with fright.
Oh my god, what a terrible night.

I dreamed, I could see you lying there.
I could see you crying there.

I could see the pain you were in.
I could feel the pain you're in.

I wanted to go and comfort you.
I wanted to go and hold on to you.

All this time you stayed away.
I couldn't do it.
I just stayed away.

I stood there, completely amazed.
I stood there full of shame.

I couldn't believe the way you cried.
I was so ashamed I could've died.

All this time, the doubt in my head.
All this time, should've come to an end.

One of these days we'll be together again.
Then I can take away the pain you're in.

Home on the Shore

Give me a log home on the shore of a lake.
With mountains so high they touch the sky.
And the bank of a stream near by.

The mountains are for us to see.
The stream is for you the lake is for me.

Where from our door we can watch an eagle soar.
Glide and circle all through the day.
Soaring up high looking for prey.

With a summer breeze rustling the trees.
The fresh mountain air, we could see a bear.

As the season changed with frost in the air.
Fall colors start to appear.

The bugle of the elk all through the day.
They may bugle and fight all through the night.

Then comes the clash of the big horn sheep.
The clash and bang all through the day as they fight for the right.
As they fight into the night.

With the mountain snow.
The wind starts to blow.
All of the animals start to go low,
they all head for the valley below.

As the deer, elk and moose head down to lower ground.
We can see them from our door of our home on the shore.

We will see all of them. The cunning wolf.
The mighty grizzly bear.
The secretive mountain lion hiding there.

From our home on the shore.
Everything nature has to adore.
We will see that and so much more.

Called True

Look in my eyes.
What do you see?
It's just some of our history.

Look again, there's something there.
It's a special love that you should see.

The feelings I feel are just for you.
I hope you know they are special and true.

It's made up above and comes from the heart.
It's something special.
It's this special thing called love.

When it's shared between the two.
It's a fantastic feeling too.

I can't explain how it feels.
There's nothing like it.
It comes to your heart.

You feel like you can never part.
If you do, it hurts your heart.

If it's true, you will survive.
You just wait and count the days.
Hold the good times close at hand.

Remember he's your loving man.
He is your world, and you are his.
This thing is called true love.
It is made from up above.

I Left Town

I look into her eyes.
There it is.
That really special kind of love.
I could tell, I could see, she was going to be special to me.
I looked again just to see.
If there was anything else for me.
They were beautiful and brown, they glisten with tears.
I could tell right away.
Something else was there that day.
Those beautiful eyes were shining at me.
I could see she was there for me.
For all the times I had to leave town.
She just waited patiently.
She never let me down.
She waited after I left town.

Soft Blue Eyes

Soft blue eyes, sensual lips.

Long blond hair and fantastic hips.

Legs that go from earth to heaven.

Silky smooth skin.

Soft hands and a loving touch.

Great mom and a great partner.

Great spouse and, yes, a fantastic wife.

Twenty-five years of wedded bliss.

Until the day you changed all of this.

All that's left is the memories of what used to be.

For you and for me.

Sit and Grieve

Pain and fear I live each day.
Trying to get rid of this memory.

It stays with me every day.
It just won't go away.

Why did this happen to us?
What caused this terrible fuss?

I know what I did to rip us apart.
I know I broke your loving heart.

I live these days full of guilt and fear.
These feelings are ripping me apart.
I wish so much that you were near.

Why can't this just go away?
Why does it get worse every day?

It's been a long time, and you still own my heart.
Someday I'll die from what I did to take us apart.
Then finally the pain in my heart will start to ease.

Then the tears may go away.
I live with this each and every day.

Until then I'll just sit and grieve.
Over the love that I lost one night.

The night I started the pain in me.
The night I set you free.

What You Had

I asked you to be with me.
I asked you to come live with me.
I asked you to marry me.

To be my wife, my lover, my best friend.
It seems you did not hear me or listen to a single thing I said.

So I sit here today dreaming that someday you'll realize what I said.

That you'll want to be with me, to marry me and be that friend.

Am I just dreaming and wishing for something
that will never come true.

Is it over? Are we through?
Or is it the fact that I'm still in love with you?

Maybe someday it will dawn on you.
Then you'll realize what you had.
Then you'll realize it wasn't that bad.

Rocky Mountain Beauty

There's nothing more beautiful to me.
Than the rocky mountain scenery.
Rugged, majestic, beautiful, and tall.

I would love to hike and hunt them all.
Central Arizona is a sight to behold.

The rugged grandeur, the beauty of it all.
From the sheer rock walls.
To the tall pine trees.
Crystal-clear rivers, creeks, and streams.

I truly cannot describe the beauty I see.
It is just absolutely beautiful and wonderful to see.

As I truck across this great nation of ours.
The Rocky Mountains are my favorite by far.

True Love

I sit here thinking of you.

Wonder what I should do.

The things I've done to repair what we had.

All I've done is make you mad.

Why can't you understand what I'm really trying to do.

I've never meant to hurt you.

It's all I can do to live without you.

You're my morning and evening thought.

The thoughts that bring the pain to me.

Each and every day of the week.

How can I make it go away.

Could you love me anyway?

Is there any love left for me in you?

Did I destroy what I meant to you?

How can you beat a love so true?

These feelings I have for you.

I really wish you were feeling them too.

I wish you could see in my heart.

I'm sure we would never part.

The love we had was made up above.

The kind of thing they call *true love*.

I Met

I met a girl a long time ago.
I fell in love, this I know.

I met her one April night.
I truly believe it was love at first sight.

We had a lot of great times, her and I.
There was something else I had to try.

I had to know if there was anything left.
Between my ex and me.
I had to check, I had to see.

I was just divorced back then.
I was scared, could not let her in.

It didn't take long for me to know.
I was so sad I had let her go.

I tried too hard to fix it with her.
She was hurt, she was scared.

I still tried in vain, I see.
I just chased her away from me.

She said she wanted to go very slow.
I pushed too hard, she finally said no.

So I sit and wonder why.
Is she with another guy?

It's been so long since I've held her tight.
I would love to hold her tonight.

To wrap her in a loving embrace.
To kiss the tears from her face.

To make the nightmares go away.
To love her for always and always to stay.

These are just dreams to me.
She said, "No, just leave me be."

There are times I want to go find her.
Look into her beautiful eyes.
To let her see, as she looks at me.

The eyes are the gateway to the soul.
I am still hers my heart and soul.

These poems I write are mostly to her.
Maybe someday my dreams will come true.
It would start with a call from you.

It's how I feel every night and day.
It's so strange I feel this way.

I live a dream of being with her again.
To love, to hold, to be her friend.

Fade Away

The other day I sent the message to you.
Then I sent you a poem or two.

I asked you what you thought.
And if they brought tears to you.

You couldn't take the time to answer me.
I don't know what to do.
Should I keep trying or should I give up on you?

I know I can, yes, I do.
I can find someone new.
The trouble is, I'm still in love with you.
I don't want someone new.

I guess the problem is, I don't know what to do.
One of these days I'll face the truth.
Just turn and walk away from you.

I guess we will both lose on that day.
The love we shared, and how we cared, will just fade away.

I'm sure it will stay with both of us buried deep inside.
We both will carry it in our hearts until we die.
As the truth comes to me.
We were just not meant to be.

Admire and Memories

I saw you walking there.
Your beautiful eyes, your beautiful hair.

I didn't think it was fair.
I just sat there and watched as you passed by.

I just admired you across the room.
I don't believe you noticed me.

All the memories came rushing back.
I prayed you would want me back.

I sat there across the room.
I couldn't stay, I had to go.
So I crept out and started slow.
I didn't know where to go.

So I headed home and drove real slow.
I couldn't see the road, for the tears in my eyes.
You looked happy with that other guy.

I'm a man I cannot cry.
The pain was so intense.
I thought that I would die.
That hurts so bad to see you with another guy.

I've thought about you for so long.
I've dreamed of the day we would meet again.
I so want to hold you again.

Star-Filled Night

I made a wish last night.
I wished upon a star.
In a star-filled night.

Which was mainly a wish for you.
A wish that will probably never come true.

I don't know where you are.
Or where you want to be.
I just truly wish you were sitting next to me.

As I sat there gazing at the star-filled night.
My mind is full of wonder, my heart full of fright.

Is that the reason I stared at the star-filled night?
I wished for you with all my might.
I wished it could come true that very night.

Maybe someday my wish could come true.
That wish is only for you.
In fact, I wished all night.
I also prayed as I stared at the star-filled night.

Is there a chance you were wishing too?
Did you wish on that same star that night.
Could this wish be one and the same.
Does that star have a name?

Complete Me

Girlfriend and I are gone again.
Making a living on the road again.

Seeing all the beautiful places we have.
Some are great.
Some are nice.
Some are a disappointment.
Just like life.

Life is what we put into it.
Live it, love it, and laughter is the key.

Put it together; it's the life for me.
I live the life in the things I do.
Places I've been.
The things I've done

I love the life, I live each day.
I laugh often throughout the day.

I love to travel this great land.
I just need a girl to travel with me.

To see the places there are to see.
To live and love and to be with me.

If this ever happens, I'll be free.
Of the feelings I hold inside of me.

Then just maybe, I'll be free.
Then my life will be complete.
Yes, the right lady will complete me.

Beautiful to See

I went for a walk the other day.
I parked my truck and started to play.
It was a clear crisp morning as I recall.
Parked so deep in the mountains so tall.

As I hiked up the hill, I saw it there.
A hidden jewel of water there.
As the sun shined on the sparkling lake.
I headed downhill to the shore.

A sandy beach I saw over there.
As I crawl through the brush and reach the beach.
That breathtaking sight I had to reach.

With mountains around so magnificent and tall.
I just sat on the beach and looked at it all.
I spent the afternoon enjoying the sight.

I had no water on that hot summer day, the
lake was cool enticing to swim.

I spent the rest of the day writing there.
Enjoying the scenery of the mountains so tall.

Girlfriend was waiting in the parking lot.
It was time to go in spite of it all.
As I headed back up to the ridge.

I stopped one more time to look around.
I'll never forget the scenery I saw.
The beautiful mountains so magnificent and tall.

Girlfriend was waiting, ready to go.
We headed back west and to work again.
The day was so enjoyable, I'll never forget that jewel of a lake.

As I sit here hours later and remember the day.
That hidden lake was magnificent to see.
A jewel of nature and beautiful to see.

Hidden in the Trees

I was trucking in Wyoming a few days back.

I had extra time, so I parked girlfriend and grabbed for my pack.

As I hiked up the hill, so majestic and tall, the
mountains are beautiful this time of fall.

I found a game trail, as I hiked up a hill, came
around the corner, and stood perfectly still.

My eyes were filled with a beautiful sight. A
shimmering waterfall sparkled with light.

I hiked to the falls and sat on a rock. I couldn't believe
the beauty, the tranquility, the peace of it all.

With the roar of the water, the wind in the trees,
this beautiful sound just put me at ease.

I sat on a rock and started to think. It was
a warm day; I wanted a drink.

The water from the falls so cold so clear. No
taste, no odor; it was perfectly clear.

I walked to the rock and wrote for a while. As I
looked at the forest and saw through the trees.

The sky was so blue it contrasted the trees. This
beautiful place is a gift from above.

Nature is beautiful a gift from God. I spent
the afternoon at peace in the trees.

The waterfall put me completely at ease. It
was getting late; it was time to go.

I had to stop and get one more look at it all.

As I climbed up the hill and found the trail
around the corner and back down the hill.

Girlfriend was waiting for me in the lot, a
welcome sight I forget her not.

Back in the seat and time to go, as I drove
through evening and most of the night.

Completely at ease, that beautiful waterfall hidden in the trees.

About the Author

Lance Figgins has been in the trucking industry his whole life. He started riding with his father in the summers as a young boy. His parents eventually opened up a trucking company called Figgins Transport. He drove long and short hauls also dispatched and helped manage the company for 30 years. When his parents retired, Lance decided to purchase his own truck and drive full time. His wife left him and he began to write down his feelings and thoughts. He soon discovered he had a talent because his friends were telling him the writing isn't just his feelings they are poetic and enjoyable to read. He then started to look for a publisher. His first book was released in August of 2015. He is still trucking today. Him and girlfriend (his truck) travel all over the U.S. and Canada. Lance enjoys writing, he continues to find depth and sincerity in love, treasures, trucking, hunting and drag racing. His daily life is looking through a windshield. His observations give clarity of emotion and serenity in the words he writes. His deepest hope is that everyone will enjoy the simplicity of life, love and laughter.

CPSIA information can be obtained
at www.ICGtesting.com
Printed in the USA
FSOW04n1636071016
25784FS

9 781683 489696